11-10

W9-BDN-439

ALL ABOUT SLEEP
FROM A TO Zzzz

VIKING

by **Elaine Scott**

Illustrated by **John O'Brien**

VIKING
Published by Penguin Group
Penguin Young Readers Group, 345 Hudson Street, New York, New York 10014, U.S.A.
Penguin Group (Canada), 90 Eglinton Avenue East, Suite 700, Toronto, Ontario, Canada M4P 2Y3
(a division of Pearson Penguin Canada Inc.)
Penguin Books Ltd, 80 Strand, London WC2R 0RL, England
Penguin Ireland, 25 St Stephen's Green, Dublin 2, Ireland (a division of Penguin Books Ltd)
Penguin Group (Australia), 250 Camberwell Road, Camberwell, Victoria 3124, Australia
(a division of Pearson Australia Group Pty Ltd)
Penguin Books India Pvt Ltd, 11 Community Centre, Panchsheel Park, New Delhi – 110 017, India
Penguin Group (NZ), 67 Apollo Drive, Rosedale, North Shore 0632, New Zealand
(a division of Pearson New Zealand Ltd)
Penguin Books (South Africa) (Pty) Ltd, 24 Sturdee Avenue, Rosebank, Johannesburg 2196, South Africa

Penguin Books Ltd, Registered Offices: 80 Strand, London WC2R 0RL, England

First published in 2008 by Viking, a division of Penguin Young Readers Group

1   3   5   7   9   10   8   6   4   2

Text copyright © Elaine Scott, 2008
Illustrations copyright © John O'Brien, 2008
All rights reserved

LIBRARY OF CONGRESS CATALOGING-IN-PUBLICATION DATA
Scott, Elaine, date—
All about sleep from a to zzzz / by Elaine Scott ; illustrations by John O'Brien.
p. cm.
ISBN 978-0-670-06188-4 (hardcover)
1. Sleep—Juvenile literature. I. O'Brien, John, date— II. Title.
QP425.S382 2008
612.8'21—dc22
2008006074

Manufactured in China   Set in Centaur MT   Book design by Jim Hoover

"I lie down and sleep; I wake again,
for the Lord sustains me."
Psalms 4:5

To my dear friend Thomas L. Steinbach, M.D.,
who cares for body and soul —E.S.

For Tess —J.O.

Acknowledgments

I am, as usual, grateful to my editor, Janet Pascal, for her wise suggestions and expert help in shaping the manuscript into a readable and accessible form. And my thanks also go to Jim Hoover, an art director who constantly shows his versatility as he creates beautiful books. And to John O'Brien for the amazing and amusing illustrations—you're a genius. Thanks, too, to my amazing husband, Parker, who is the boy who lost his hatchet, and also the boy who walked into the snow. (And posthumous thanks to his father, William Scott, for rescuing him, so I could later marry him.) Finally, I owe deep thanks to my friend Tom Steinbach, M.D., for his expert reading of the text.

Contents

Introduction

LATE AT NIGHT on Saturday, June 25, 2005, a fifteen-year-old girl left her house near London, England. She walked to a nearby construction site, climbed to the top of a 130-foot crane, walked along its narrow beam, and curled up on a concrete counterweight at its end. She wasn't frightened. And she wasn't reckless. She was just asleep. Fortunately, a passerby on a late-night stroll saw the girl and called the authorities. A fireman carefully crawled along the beam until he reached her. Then he woke her, wrapped her in a safety harness, and helped her get down.

Fifty years earlier, in Grapevine, Texas, a ten-year-old boy playing in the woods lost his toy hatchet. Although he searched for it for several days, he could never find it. Finally, he gave up. Two years later, the boy had a dream. In it, he could "see" the small hatchet—and where it lay buried. The following morning, hardly daring to believe his dream, he hurried to the place he had dreamed about. He began to scrape away two years' worth of dried leaves, twigs, and dirt; and there was the hatchet—exactly where he had dreamed it would be.

Even though most people don't walk in their sleep, and plenty of lost objects stay lost and are never found, these true stories point out that sleeping isn't simply losing touch with the daytime world. Unlike the girl who climbed the crane, most of us remain in bed while we sleep. But, like the boy who dreamed of his lost hatchet, we have *something* happening in our brains while we're sleeping. Sleep is a complicated—even mysterious—process. What is it? Where do we go when we go to sleep?

Scientists around the world are studying sleep, asking questions and getting answers. Those answers often lead to more questions. Sleep remains a mystery that is just beginning to be solved.

CHAPTER ONE
Everything Sleeps

FRUIT FLIES SLEEP. So do giraffes. Some birds can sleep while they fly. And dolphins can sleep with one eye open and keep on swimming! Although this is a book about human sleep, the truth is, every creature on Earth—and even some plants—sleep.

The definition of "sleep" differs, however, depending on what kind of animal you are talking about. Animals with large brains—such as humans or dogs—can have their brain waves measured to tell if they are asleep. They exhibit behaviors that show they are asleep, too. For example, most people—and lots of animals—sleep lying down. Most of us don't move very much while we sleep. Low noises don't wake us up. However, a sleeping dog, cat, or person can be wakened by a loud noise or a touch, which is one way sleep is different from being in a coma or under anesthesia. In those states, no stimulation from the outside world wakes us up.

Scientists can understand a lot about sleep in humans and other animals with large brains, because they know how to measure electrical activity in their brains. However, reptiles and other amphibians don't have large brains, so scientists have been unable to detect the same kind of brain waves in them. And yet we know that alligators and other reptiles rest in a way that looks like sleep, even if it's more like "zoning out" than real sleep.

Green plants "sleep" at night by folding their leaves and closing tiny pores, called stomata, that are on the undersides of the leaves. During the day, the stomata open to take in sunlight and carbon dioxide while they release oxygen. The sunlight, carbon dioxide, and water from the plant's stem combine to create sugar. At night, the process stops. While the plant "sleeps," the sugar gets turned into starch so the plants can store it. Later it will become fats and protein—plant food! This process is called photosynthesis, which is a Greek word that means "combining with light."

The average healthy person spends 8 hours a day asleep. That adds up to *2,920 hours a year.* So if a person lived to be seventy-five, that person would have spent twenty-five of those years sleeping. That's a third of a lifetime, which would be a long time to be doing nothing. But are you doing nothing when you sleep? Science says no. While your body may be still and you are not aware of your surroundings, your brain is still busy.

Long before science was part of the human experience, ancient teachers and philosophers were interested in sleep; and though they didn't know what sleep was, they had some wild guesses! A Greek physician named Alcmaeon, who lived in the sixth century BC, believed that people fell asleep because all the blood had drained from their heads. Two hundred years later, in the fourth century BC, the great Greek philosopher Aristotle decided sleep had something to do with heat sinking into the middle of the body during digestion. Using something most people have noticed to support his idea, he wrote, "Sleep is most oppressive in its onset after meals"—that is, a big meal makes you sleepy.

For centuries after Aristotle, teachers and philosophers thought about sleep. They wanted to know why we fell asleep and why we woke up. They wanted to know more about dreams—the good ones and the scary ones, too. They wondered why some people walked in their sleep and others stayed in bed, and they offered different answers to these questions. However, in those ancient days everyone seemed to agree on one thing—sleeping had something to do with the heart, because they believed the heart controlled everything in the body.

It wasn't until the 1400s, in a period known as the Renaissance, that people began to understand that it's the brain that controls our bodies, not the heart. But that discovery, while important, still did not explain why or how humans—or animals—fell asleep. What was the brain actually doing? Time passed and scientists continued to work on the answer.

In the late nineteenth and early twentieth centuries, some researchers thought that sleep was caused by either too much or too little blood getting to the brain. Others said sleep happened because there wasn't enough oxygen getting there. Still more claimed that chemicals such as carbon dioxide or even cholesterol built up in our bodies during the day; and when too much of these substances was present in our blood, we fell asleep. Then, while we slept, the chemicals gradually drained away—and when they were gone, we woke up. None of these theories—or ideas—was right; however, the early researchers were correct about one thing. Chemicals do play a role in putting us to sleep and in waking us up again.

Scientists may have disagreed on *how* we go to sleep, but for most of the history of sleep research, they agreed that nothing much happened *while* we slept. They believed that during sleep, the brain stopped most of its activity—with the exception of dreaming, which they also did not understand. A sleeping person, scientists said, was in a state somewhere between being awake and being dead. That theory wasn't right, either.

CHAPTER TWO
It's All in Your Head

EVERYONE AGREES THAT sleep is necessary—as necessary as food and water. In fact, sleep is so important that sleep deprivation—not letting someone sleep for long periods—is considered a form of torture. Menachem Begin, who was prime minister of Israel from 1977 to 1983, was a prisoner of war in Russia as a young man. He endured sleep deprivation during questioning. He wrote about the experience in his book *White Nights: The Story of a Prisoner in Russia.* "In the head of the interrogated prisoner, a haze begins to form. His spirit is wearied to death, his legs are unsteady, and he has one sole desire: to sleep. . . . Anyone who has experienced this desire knows that even hunger and thirst are not comparable with it."

After going just three days without sleep, people can begin to hallucinate and see things that aren't really there.

They lose the ability to think and reason. They often become afraid—even if there is nothing to fear. Their eyes hurt. They don't want to eat. When they talk, they often don't make sense. For a person who has gone without it for a few days, nothing matters more than going to sleep.

Some people lose the ability to sleep at all, no matter how tired they are. Patients with the illness called fatal familial insomnia may go for months with no sleep. Eventually, the lack of sleep kills them.

Fortunately, that disease is rare. And most people do not go for days without sleep—they go to bed every night. But what about people who sleep poorly? Or those who don't sleep enough? They suffer real consequences, too. They get sick more easily. They find it harder to concentrate, and harder to learn. People who don't get enough sleep can be difficult to get along with, too. Cranky people are often sleepy people.

So your body needs sleep. But the question remains: What is sleep? And what makes it happen?

Falling asleep and waking up happens to your entire body, but the process begins in the brain. Therefore, in order to understand anything about sleep, you have to understand something about the brain.

Our brains are about the size of a cantaloupe and are wrinkled like a walnut. They weigh about three pounds and are 75 percent water. Human brains are the most complex, mysterious, and marvelous organs on this planet. With their 100 billion various cells, our brains make it possible for us to, among other things, think, learn, love, fear, walk, talk, see, hear, touch, taste, smell, breathe—and sleep.

The human brain is divided into three major sections: the forebrain, the midbrain, and the brain stem. Think of the brain stem as the stalk of the brain, a little like the stalk on a head of broccoli. The brain stem connects the spinal cord to the rest of the brain. Together, the brain and the spinal cord form our central nervous system.

The nerve cells in our central nervous system are activated by electrically charged chemicals called neurotransmitters. *Neuro* is Greek for "nerve"; and when we transmit something, we send it. So a neurotransmitter is a nerve-signaling chemical. Depending on what kind of nerves are stimulated, the body's reaction is different. Neurotransmitters signal some nerves to move the muscles that allow us to run, talk, laugh, or cry. And other neurotransmitters stimulate the areas of the brain that keep us awake or put us to sleep.

The existence of neurotransmitters was proved by an experiment from a dream. According to Austrian scientist Dr. Otto Loewi, "In the night of Easter Saturday, 1921, I awoke, turned on the light, and jotted down a few notes on a tiny slip of paper. Then I fell asleep again." The following morning, Dr. Loewi couldn't read his own handwriting. He tried to remember his dream, but he could not. However, the next night he woke again, and he suddenly remembered. He had dreamed of an experiment using two frog hearts. Not wanting to forget again, Dr. Loewi immediately got up, went to his laboratory, and performed the experiment, which was successful. Dr. Loewi's discovery of neurotransmitters was so important that in 1936 he was awarded the Nobel Prize in Medicine for his work.

Different neurotransmitters play a role in keeping us awake or putting us to sleep. Some neurotransmitters stimulate "awake" neurons, and we respond by being awake and alert, ready for the day's activities. Others stimulate "sleep-on" neurons, which make us go to sleep.

When we feel sleepy, researchers believe, a combination of chemicals, neurotransmitters, and hormones is responsible. During the day, a chemical in our blood called adenosine builds up. When the chemical level of adenosine gets high enough in the bloodstream, it makes us feel sleepy. Then as night approaches, neurotransmitters block, or "turn off," the "awake" neurons and stimulate the "sleep-on" neurons. During the day, our body's supply of a hormone called melatonin has been decreasing. At night, our internal clock tells the body to start producing melatonin again. The rising levels of the chemical adenosine, the sudden increase in the level of the hormone melatonin, and the neurotransmitters turning off the "awake" neurons and turning on the "sleep-on" neurons all work together to put us to sleep.

Though there is still much to learn about why we fall asleep and why we wake, we know that chemicals, hormones, and neurotransmitters definitely play a key role in the process. And we also know that while these elements in our bodies may control *why* we sleep, it is light that controls *when*.

CHAPTER THREE
Days and Nights

MOST PEOPLE, and many other animals, are diurnal creatures. That means they sleep at night and remain awake during the day. This pattern is not an accident or a choice. Our bodies rest at night due to something called circadian rhythms. *Circa* means "around" in Latin and *dia* comes from the word for "day," so the term circadian rhythms describes how our bodies respond to the cycle of light and darkness during the course of one full day and night. Circadian rhythms are what power the "biological clock" that helps control when we fall asleep and when we wake up. Every person's biological clock is slightly different. Some people like to stay up late, and others love to get to bed early. It just depends on how their biological clock is "set."

Many animals, such as owls and bats, are nocturnal, which means they sleep during the day and are awake during the night. Their circadian rhythms are just the opposite of human rhythms. Other creatures, such as cats, rattlesnakes, and porcupines, are crepuscular, which means they are most active and awake at dawn and dusk, when they hunt for food.

Different animals have different biological clocks, and different animals need varying amounts of sleep. For example, a giraffe needs only two hours of sleep a night, a human being needs about eight hours, and a bat sleeps for twenty.

Our biological clock gets "set" by light. When light enters our eyes, it is transmitted through the retina, a layer of nerve cells that clings to the back of the eyeball. Then neurotransmitters send the message through the optic nerve and on to a group of nerves that are clustered deep inside a pea-sized part of the brain called the hypothalamus. This cluster of nerves, called the suprachiasmatic nucleus, or SCN for short, forms the body's internal clock. When the SCN receives the signal that it is light, it resets itself, and the body is ready for a new day. Light also makes the levels of that sleep-producing hormone, melatonin, decrease during the day.

In fact, our internal clock is so sensitive to light that if we waken in the night and turn on a bright light, we may have trouble falling back asleep again. Why? Because our "clock" perceives that light as daylight and tells the body it's time to wake up. For this reason, a dark room helps most people sleep better.

However, if a person spends several days in a dark room with no watch or clock to tell time, that person will begin

to "free run," which means they will fall asleep and wake up according to their internal biological clock. People whose sleep is free running may discover that it takes their bodies about twenty-five hours to cycle through a "day" rather than the sun's twenty-four-hour day. Many "free-run" sleepers say they feel more refreshed by their sleep than those who go to sleep and wake up at times determined by the clock. However, since the world runs on a twenty-four-hour day, it is hard for most people to allow themselves free-run sleep.

> *Scientists working on the Mars robotic rovers discovered what it feels like to adapt to a longer day, because a Martian day, or sol, lasts 24 hours and 39 minutes. At first, they continued to think in terms of Earth's 24-hour day. This meant that in order to work during Martian daylight hours, they had to go to work at 8:00 a.m. one day, 8:39 the following day, 9:18 the next, and so forth. So they abandoned Earth time. Instead, even though they were on Earth, they lived on Martian time, wearing watches and using clocks that had been specially made to mark off a 24-hour-and-39-minute day.*

There are those, however, who because of illness or injury have had damage to their SCN. Their sleep will be free running, whether they want it to be or not, because their biological clocks cannot reset themselves. The world operates on a twenty-four-hour day, so it can be difficult for free-run sleepers to work a set schedule, since their bodies want to sleep and wake up at odd times. Sadly, most—though not all—people who are blind have trouble sleeping; and they will free run, too, because their brains cannot perceive light. However, experiments have demonstrated that some forms of blindness still allow signals from light to reach the brain. If that is the case, the person—though blind—will still have normal waking and sleeping cycles.

Some people work at night and sleep during the day, and that kind of schedule can *really* upset a person's biological clock. Research shows that people who work at night have a higher rate of accidents and can have a number of other problems, such as not being able to concentrate on their work as well as they would like. In the absence of sunlight, bright artificial light can help a person's biological clock adjust to the change in natural circadian rhythms.

If a space mission launches in the middle of the night, the astronauts need to reset their biological clocks so they will be wide-awake at launch. So during their week of quarantine, before a mission, the astronauts adjust their circadian rhythms by exposing themselves to timed doses of bright light.

Travel can also disturb our circadian rhythms— especially if we cross several time zones in one day. Our internal clock can do a good job of keeping up with slight changes in our body's rhythm, so if we cross one time zone, we usually don't notice it, because we are only losing or gaining one hour. But if we cross several time zones, as people do when they fly across an entire ocean or continent, our internal clock can get upset.

For example, if you flew from New York to London, the flight should last about seven hours. So if you took off at 6:30 p.m., you would land in London at about 1:30 a.m. by your body's internal clock. That's past midnight, and you would be *tired.* There would be a lot of adenosine building up in your body, you would experience a surge in melatonin production, and neurotransmitters would be working hard to turn off your "awake" neurons and activate your "sleep-on" neurons. Your body thinks it's night and wants to sleep, but because of time differences it would only be 6:30 in the morning in London. In order to adjust to London time, you try to stay awake; but if you manage to stay awake until 7:30 p.m., you will have been awake for twenty hours since boarding your flight in New York. This kind of weariness is called jet lag. It can take a few days on either end of the trip to get over it.

CHAPTER FOUR
Amazing
Measuring Machines

NEW INFORMATION ABOUT
sleep—and what happens while we sleep—is being
discovered every day. One of the many things scientists have learned is that the brain is an electrochemical
organ. That means that chemicals in the brain can produce
electricity—not a lot, but enough to power a ten-watt
lightbulb. The electricity moves between areas of the brain
in a series of wavelike impulses called brain waves.

Researchers have invented machines that can measure
brain activity. These machines have helped scientists understand even more about what happens when we sleep.
Like a lot of other things in medicine and research, these
machines have long names—the electroencephalograph
(EEG, for short), the electromyograph (EMG), and the
electrooculograph (EOG). To use them, researchers attach
electrodes to a subject's body. (It doesn't hurt.) The subject

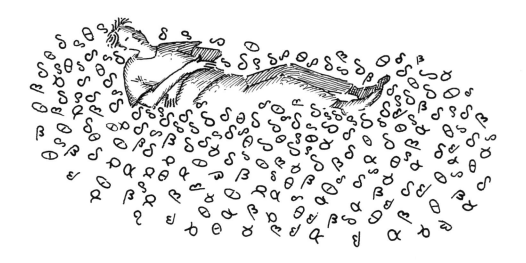

falls asleep, and the EEG measures brain waves, the EMG measures muscle activity, and the EOG measures the sleeping person's eye movements. The information comes out as wavy lines on a piece of paper.

By using the EEG, sleep researchers have discovered that our brains produce four distinct kinds of brain waves. Each wave is named after a letter in the Greek alphabet. There are beta waves (β), alpha waves (α), theta waves (θ), and delta waves (δ). Together, these waves control how aware and awake we are.

Beta waves are the fastest brain waves. If you are paying attention in school, your brain is flooded with beta waves. If you argue with someone, or you're frightened or excited and happy, you are also in a beta-wave state. Anyone who is awake and alert is producing a lot of beta waves in their brain.

Alpha waves are the second-fastest brain waves. Alpha waves occur when a person is awake but completely relaxed. For example, if you stopped to watch the sun set or tried to find pictures in the clouds on a summer afternoon, your brain would probably produce a lot of alpha waves. People who pray, meditate, or just sit quietly letting their thoughts wander are also in an alpha-wave state.

Have you ever bounced a ball repeatedly, or run around a track, and found your thoughts wandering to other things? When that happens, theta waves are flooding your brain. They are even slower than alpha waves. Theta waves usually dominate your brain when you're doing something that is repetitive and automatic—something that doesn't require much concentration. People often report getting new and creative ideas during this period.

And then there is the fourth brain-wave state—delta. These are the slowest brain waves your body produces. Delta waves are present when you fall into a deep, dreamless sleep.

Beta, alpha, theta, and delta brain waves are all always present in your brain, though one or another of them is usually dominant. So while you are reading this book, you can be sure that your brain is creating lots of beta waves; but there are also small traces of alpha, theta, and delta waves firing, too. And all of them play a role in falling—and staying—asleep.

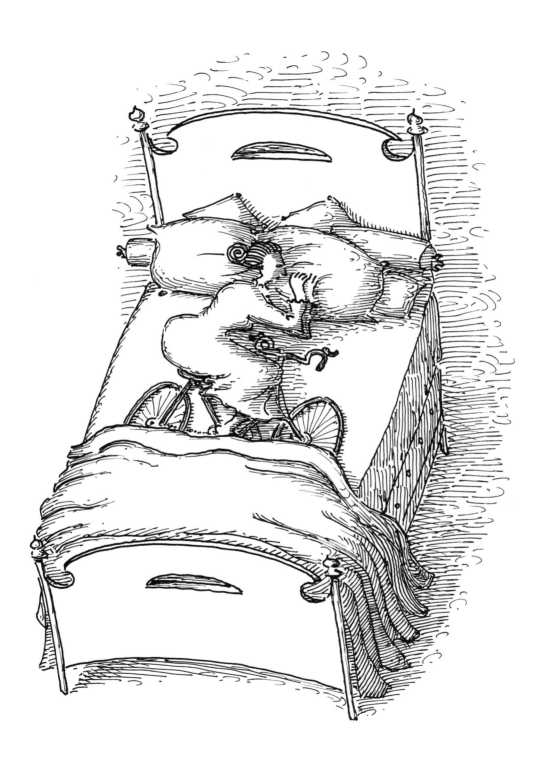

CHAPTER FIVE

Where Do We Go When We Go to Sleep?

RESEARCH USING THE EEG, EMG, and EOG machines has helped doctors understand that we don't really just fall asleep—we slip into it. Sleeping is a process that takes place over five stages.

Everyone knows when the first stage of sleep is setting in. You feel tired. Because you're tired, your breathing becomes shallow. If your breaths are light and shallow for too long, the brain may send a signal that it needs oxygen—and you yawn. After a few good yawns, your eyes may get heavy and your head may nod. You begin to feel groggy and less aware of your surroundings. You are deeply relaxed. At this point, if you close your eyes for a few minutes you will fall into stage 1 sleep, which is also called light sleep. Your beta and alpha waves are lessening, and the theta and delta waves are increasing. But in stage 1 sleep it is still easy to wake you up. And

if that happens, your beta waves will increase again.

Some people experience a falling sensation when they are in stage 1 sleep—then they wake up with a jerk. Doctors call this sensation a hypnic jerk, and it's perfectly normal. They don't know for sure what causes it. But they have an idea. Muscles relax as the body gets ready for deeper sleep. Most scientists believe that—for an instant—the brain thinks the relaxed muscles will let the body fall down. To prevent the "fall," the brain sends a signal to the arms and legs, telling them to thrash around in an attempt to keep the body balanced. Of course, it is the thrashing that wakes the sleeping person—often with a jerk. Once the brain realizes there is no danger, stage 2 sleep follows quickly.

Stage 2 is deeper sleep. Your body is relaxed, and your brain is disconnecting from the outside world. Theta waves are taking over. During stage 2 sleep, your brain also creates something called sleep spindles. A sleep spindle is a sudden burst of electrical activity in the brain. It shows up as a spindle, or spike, on the EEG record. Doctors believe that sleep spindles help you disconnect from the noises of the outside world by interfering with the way the brain processes sounds.

You stay in stage 2 sleep for about fifteen minutes, and then you slip into stage 3. During this stage, the strong and slow delta waves are taking over from the theta waves. Your brain is resting, and you're not processing much information at all. When nearly all your brain activity is measured in delta waves, you move into stage 4 sleep.

During stages 3 and 4, which are often called deep sleep, you are *really* relaxed! Your mind is quiet, your eyes don't move, your muscles are loose, and your heartbeat and breathing are slow and regular. It can be hard for someone to wake you up during slow-wave sleep, and if you are awakened, you may move very slowly and appear confused.

Everyone needs plenty of slow-wave sleep. It's important, because this is the period when our bodies rest and heal. The pineal gland deep in the brain produces growth hormones during slow-wave sleep. In children, growth hormones encourage bone and muscle development, and in adults the same hormones work on repairing tissues that have broken down. Sleep studies indicate that people who do not get enough of this deep, restful sleep over a period of several days often feel tired all the time. Some feel ill—they may even *become* ill. Some have reported feeling sad or depressed. Still others say they feel angry—and it's all because they couldn't rest well at night.

But most people do experience periods of slow-wave sleep; and after a person has been in deep sleep for about an hour, the brain is ready for stage 5, or REM, sleep. REM stands for "rapid eye movement," and that's exactly what happens when we reach this level of sleep. Our eyes move rapidly, as if we were "watching" our dreams play out like a movie against the backs of our closed eyelids.

Scientists are learning that sleep phases may play an important role in converting short-term memories into long-term memories. A short-term memory is information that you hold in your brain for a short period of time and then it's gone. Long-term memories, on the other hand, are information that is stored forever and can be used again and again. For example, if someone asked you to multiply 9 times 18 in your head (no paper and pencil to help!) your short-term memory will hold the numbers 9 and 18 in your brain, while your long-term memory recalls the multiplication tables so you can multiply 9 times 10 and 9 times 8. Then your short-term memory takes over again, holding the results of the multiplication you just did, while your long-term memory does the addition necessary to come up with the right answer—which is 162. Half an hour later, however, you probably won't even remember what numbers you were asked to multiply.

We need both short- and long-term memories in order to function in life. All information goes into short-term memory first. Then, while we sleep, our brains go to work. Some of the information is discarded, but most of it is kept and turned into long-term memories that we don't forget—at least not right away.

Vocabulary words, piano scales, and how to ride a bike are just some of the long-term memories that are sealed in our brains with a good night's sleep. And the opposite is true, too. Research has shown that if a person gets less than six hours of sleep in a night, the ability to store long-term memories is lessened. So no matter how much you study the night before a test, if you don't get enough sleep you may have trouble remembering what you learned.

The process of sorting and storing our memories takes place during all the stages of sleep, but research seems to indicate that deep sleep is most important for remembering facts. But for how to do things, REM sleep may be more important.

> Suppose you learned to ride a bike on Wednesday but couldn't ride again until Saturday. If you slept less than six hours a night for the next three nights, on Saturday you might discover your body had "forgotten" how to ride, and you'd have to practice balance all over again.

REM sleep is the period most people find fascinating. Although brief dreams can occur in any stage of sleep, the most vivid dreams seem to happen then. You can actually see a person's eyes move during REM sleep. But the eyes are the only parts of the body that move. The rest, from the neck down, becomes, well, paralyzed. But it's only temporary.

CHAPTER SIX
Don't Get Out of Bed

REM SLEEP IS so different from the other stages of sleep that scientists often refer to it as paradoxical sleep. A paradox is a statement that seems to contradict itself. It looks as if it can't be true, but it is. For example, lots of beta waves are present when we are in REM sleep. But beta waves are the ones that are present when we are most awake. Why are they also there during REM? It's a paradox.

As we sink into REM sleep, the delta waves of deep sleep are replaced by theta waves—the ones that are present when we are drowsy. Then the theta waves give way to the wide-awake beta waves—but we remain asleep, and we begin to dream. Other changes happen during REM sleep, too. Our blood pressure increases, and more blood flows to the brain. Our hearts beat faster, and our breathing becomes shallow and irregular. Our eyes move; and

then, in the most mysterious change of all, our arms and legs become paralyzed. And like everything else that happens with sleep, this temporary paralysis—which is called atonia—begins in the brain; in this case, the brain stem. Atonia is caused by those important messengers, neurotransmitters.

While we are awake, neurotransmitters in our brain stem travel to our muscles, giving them various messages. These muscle movements are called voluntary, because we choose how, when, where, and which muscles will move. If we choose to raise our arms, move our legs, run, jump, swallow, smile, scratch our heads, or pet the dog, neurotransmitters carry the message from the brain to the appropriate body part.

However, during sleep paralysis, scientists think that these neurotransmitters are somehow "turned off." Without neurotransmitters telling our muscles to move, we remain still. Unlike the kind of paralysis that results from illness or accident, this paralysis is a good thing, because it prevents us from acting out our dreams. In fact, if someone doesn't experience paralysis during REM sleep, doctors say they have a sleeping disorder.

The disorder is called RBD, or REM behavior disorder. A person with RBD has neurotransmitters that don't turn off muscle movements. While the person sleeps, the neurotransmitters keep on working—so, for example, someone who is dreaming of playing soccer could easily get out of bed and kick the nightstand. Or a person dreaming of being in a fight could hit a roommate! (As we will see, this is not the same as sleepwalking.) Moving while dreaming can create a lot of problems.

One young man dreamed he was standing around with a group of friends, watching a baby alligator. In his dream, the baby alligator singled the man out and tried to bite him. To fend off the baby alligator attack, the man began trying to kick it away. He was awakened by a pain in his foot—not from a baby alligator bite, but because he kicked the wall so hard he pushed himself across the bed.

The paralysis that goes with REM sleep affects only our voluntary muscles, and it disappears as soon as we slip into another stage of sleep—or wake up. Another set of muscles, our involuntary ones, work all the time, whether we ask them to or not. They are not affected by sleep paralysis, so you can fall asleep knowing that your heart will keep beating and your lungs will inhale and exhale all night long. You don't have to give it a thought.

We move back and forth through the five stages of sleep throughout the night in a pattern, or sleep cycle. The first four stages of sleep take about ninety minutes to complete, followed by a period of REM sleep that usually lasts about ten minutes, so the first sleep cycle lasts about one hundred minutes. An average person may complete five sleep cycles in a night. Deep sleep, stages 3 and 4, occurs in the first two or three cycles of sleep. As we move toward morning, we spend more time in REM and stages 1 and 2 sleep. Then as morning gets closer, we may be spending as much as an hour in REM sleep. The dreams that occur during this period of REM are the easiest to remember when we wake.

Some people can't remember dreaming at all. But whether we can remember our dreams or not, most of us spend about two hours a night in this mysterious REM sleep that science is learning more about every day.

CHAPTER SEVEN

Dream On . . .

SINCE THE BEGINNING of our recorded history, human beings have talked about their dreams—and written about them, too. There are many dream stories in the Bible, as well as in ancient Greek and Roman myths. In fact, stories about dreams occur in every culture of the world.

One familiar story comes from the book of Genesis. It is about a young Hebrew man named Joseph. Joseph had a talent for interpreting dreams, though he claimed that it was God, not he, who interpreted them. The pharaoh of Egypt was having strange dreams. Seven skinny cows were eating seven fat cows, and seven fat stalks of grain were eating seven skinny stalks of grain. Joseph interpreted that dream to mean that Egypt would have seven years of plenty, followed by seven years of famine. He told the pharaoh to save food and store it during the good years, so the people would have enough to eat during the famine. Joseph was rewarded for his dream interpretation by being made an official in the pharaoh's court.

In ancient times, people often saw dreams as revelations or prophecies from their gods. The ancient Egyptians and Greeks built sleep temples, where people came to have their dreams interpreted and their diseases cured. Remember the boy who found his hatchet in a dream? Had he lived in ancient Greece, when he told others about his dream, they likely would have claimed that it had been a revelation from the gods.

Asclepios was a Greek god whose temples were dedicated to dreams used for healing. The people who came to these temples were called Seekers. The priests induced dreams in the Seekers by using a combination of chanting and magical incantations, along with medicinal herbs. Then the priest interpreted each dream and made suggestions about healing

In modern times, scientists can measure the brain waves of someone who is dreaming, but the actual dream can't be recorded on a machine and spit out as a paper record. To this day, the only record we have of a dream is the story the dreamer tells about it.

Dreams have been interpreted since ancient times, and they are still interpreted today. Many books have been written, and many Web sites created, that relate to dream interpretation. These books and Web sites are based on the idea that a symbol in a dream always means the same thing, no matter who is doing the dreaming. It's almost as if there were a dictionary of dream symbols! For example, one site states that if you dream of the letter *A*, you feel superior. Or if you dream about a mad dog, your friends are going to yell at you. These are not very scientific interpretations.

Some serious scientists are also engaged in the work of determining where dreams come from and what they could mean. One of the earliest of these scientists was Sigmund Freud, who lived in Austria from 1856 to 1939. In 1900, Dr. Freud became famous for his book *The Interpretation of Dreams*. Basically, Dr. Freud believed that a person's dreams were created in that person's mind. In other words, they were something like a thought process. He said, "The dream is instigated by the wish."

Dr. Freud believed that if you wished for something, your brain would go to work to try to make the wish come true. For example, if you saw an ice-cream store, you might wish you could have an ice-cream cone. If you went into the store and bought one, that would be the end of the story—as far as your mind was concerned. However, according to Dr. Freud's theory, if you didn't get the ice-cream cone, your desire for it wouldn't go away. It would still be there, unfulfilled, and—according to Freud—that wish would somehow have to be expressed. So perhaps at dinner you might say, "Pass the ice cream" when you meant to say, "Pass the potatoes." That kind of silly mistake is now known as a Freudian slip. Your mind still wanted that ice cream. Or your mind might try to satisfy your wish while you were asleep. Perhaps you might dream of eating an ice-cream cone, or even swimming in a pool of ice cream.

A modern (and unscientific) interpretation of a dream in which you are eating ice cream says that the dream means you are a happy person who has good luck. However, if you dream of melting ice cream, it means you have failed to reach your goals.

Today, some scientists agree with Freud that our dreams come from thought processes, while others think our dreams are rooted in something more biological—the physical working of the brain. According to the biological theory, during REM sleep, neurotransmitters in the brain stem send signals to the midbrain and forebrain. These signals contain random bits of information that the brain has collected during the day and stored in short-term memory. However, since random information doesn't have a pattern to it, it doesn't make much sense. So the brain tries to make sense of the signals it is getting by organizing the information into a dream. Since the information isn't well organized, the dream isn't, either. So a person could dream of throwing a baseball into a swimming pool while walking through school without shoes on. According to the biological theory, a dream is simply a way the brain tries to process information, and the dream doesn't have to make sense at all.

But what of those dreams that do make sense? Abraham Lincoln had a famous one. He told the dream to a friend named Ward Hill Lamon, who wrote down what the president said. "There seemed to be a death-like stillness about me. Then I heard subdued sobs, as if a number of people were weeping. . . . Before me was a catafalque, on which rested a corpse wrapped in funeral vestments. . . . 'Who is dead in the White House?' I demanded of one of the soldiers who were acting as guards. 'The President,' was his answer. 'He was killed by an assassin.'" Three days later, President Abraham Lincoln was assassinated by John Wilkes Booth.

No one can say for sure why Lincoln had this dream, but some researchers explain the mystery this way: Our brains store all kinds of information. In the case of Abraham Lincoln, he was president during the bitter civil war between the North and the South. Many people hated him and wished him dead. There had already been unsuccessful attempts on his life. Perhaps his brain called up memories of some of those attempts and translated that information into the dream—and the fact that he was killed three days later was nothing more than a coincidence. Lincoln himself believed that the dream meant nothing, though he admitted, "I have been strangely annoyed by it ever since."

In some ways, the brain can be compared to a computer. Like the files in a computer, sometimes the files in our brains get "deleted." We simply forget what we knew. Just as deleted computer files can be recovered, things we have forgotten can be brought back to our memory. So someone could explain the dream of the boy and his lost hatchet by claiming the location was always in the boy's brain; but like a lost computer file, the memory needed to be located and accessed. The dream did that, and the boy remembered where to look.

Likewise, when Dr. Loewi couldn't read his own handwriting, it took a dream to stimulate his brain and help him remember what he had written. Today, scientists would say there was nothing supernatural about the dreams of the president, the boy, or the doctor. Their dreams were a combination of the biological processes of the brain and the information stored there.

Today's research indicates that only a quarter of people's dreams are pleasant. The rest are bad dreams or even nightmares. There is a difference between a bad dream and a nightmare. A nightmare wakes you up, but you sleep through a bad dream.

According to some scientists, bad dreams may help us conquer our fears. Sleep researcher Dr. Tore Nielson says, "The brain learns quickly what to be afraid of, but if there isn't a check on the process, we'd fear things in adulthood we feared in childhood." Most of us don't fear monsters in the closet or under the bed as we grow up, and it may be that our bad dreams when we were younger have helped us face, and get over, those fears. It works the same way for adults, too. According to Dr. Nielson, bad dreams can help adults deal with their feelings of fear, frustration, or anger.

Sometimes nightmares can be helpful, too. Elias Howe, who invented the sewing machine, came up with the idea of a needle with the hole at the pointed end after he had a nightmare about being chased by warriors whose spears had a hole near the point!

Still, no one is absolutely positive why we have any kind of dream—bad or good. Perhaps we dream in order to ful-

fill wishes, as Freud said. Or maybe we dream to recapture information that is temporarily forgotten, as happened to Dr. Loewi and the boy who lost his hatchet. Or perhaps we dream to get over our fears and frustrations.

However, no matter why we dream, all researchers agree that dreams are important. In fact, if a person stops dreaming for some reason, perhaps because of illness or a medication, once dreams resume, there will be more of them, and they may be very bizarre. Our brains apparently *need* to dream, so "sweet dreams" isn't just a nice nighttime wish—it's a necessity.

CHAPTER EIGHT
Troubled Sleep

MOST CHILDREN HAVE had the dream that someone or something is chasing them. They run, but their feet won't propel them forward. And then they wake; and when parents or other adults come to comfort them, they explain what happened in their dream. Often the explanations are detailed accounts like this: *"A monster was chasing me, and he had claws and eyes that shot fire, and I ran and ran and ran, but he was always after me, and he was catching up with me, and then my feet wouldn't move anymore and he was grabbing me, and I screamed and I woke up."*

People remember their nightmares, because a nightmare wakes you up; and young children—even adults—may find it difficult to return to sleep after having one. However, a nightmare is just a dream—a bad one, to be sure, but a dream nonetheless.

There is another kind of dream that isn't just a bad dream, or even a nightmare. Remember how your body is paralyzed during REM sleep? Well, some people wake up and find themselves still paralyzed. They can't move or cry for help. To make matters worse, they may "see" alien creatures approaching them. Or they may feel a crushing sensation on their chest, as if someone were sitting there. Many people who report this crushing sensation claim it's a monster—or even an alien they "saw" coming toward them. Some people have the sensation that they have left their bodies and are floating around the room. Nothing of the kind is happening, of course. These people are just caught in a state somewhere between being asleep and being awake.

They may be able to remember the experience and describe it vividly. *"Aliens came into the room and lifted me from the bed and carried me to their spaceship and performed experiments on me"* is a common description of this kind of experience. Someone can have this kind of hallucination when they are falling asleep, or waking up. Once the person wakes up fully, the lock on their muscles gives way. They may be breathing hard, and their heart may be racing, but they are not harmed, and they do have quite a story to tell!

The English word nightmare *comes from an Anglo-Saxon word that means "an evil female spirit." Centuries ago, before anyone understood sleep, people who woke in a state of sleep paralysis feeling pressure on their chests believed that witches were sitting on them. Eventually the word* nightmare *evolved, meaning "the evil spirit who comes in the night."*

Another scary thing that occasionally happens to people when they are asleep is called sleep terror. Sleep terror is different from a nightmare. It isn't a dream. There is no "story" to it, and there are no frightening characters. A sleep terror is just a feeling. People who experience sleep terror wake up terrified. Their hearts beat fast. They might scream or cry. Even though they are sitting up in bed, it is hard to wake them up. They may resist being comforted by another person.

Unlike dreams, which happen most often during REM sleep, sleep terrors usually happen in the first half of the night, during the first periods of stages 3 and 4 deep sleep. Doctors are unsure about what causes them, but some think they may be caused by fever, not getting enough sleep, or perhaps leftover worries from the day—stress. The good news is, they only last for about fifteen minutes—then the person goes back to sleep and, chances are, won't remember the incident in the morning.

Like nightmares, sleep terrors are unpleasant. But also like nightmares, they tend to go away as a person grows up—though some adults can have sleep terrors, too.

Another problem we may have while asleep isn't quite so terrifying, but it can be annoying—especially to other people. We snore. Snoring happens when something gets in the way of air passing over the soft tissues in the mouth. Normally, we take in air through the nose and it makes its way to the lungs with no problem. However, when some people sleep, their soft tissues relax until they come so close they may touch each other, or at least drastically narrow the passageway air takes on the way to the lungs. The soft tissues of the mouth include the soft palate (the place where the roof of the mouth stops feeling solid), the uvula (which hangs down from the soft palate like a small, fleshy stalactite), the tonsils, and the tongue.

As the sleeper takes a breath and it passes through these collapsed soft tissues, the tissues vibrate and the resulting sound can range from a soft *zzzzzz* to a loud snort. Most people who snore make more noise when they are inhaling than when they are exhaling. And many more adults snore than children. Snoring is only annoying to someone who has to listen to it. It doesn't hurt the person who is sleeping. But snoring can be very loud. The loudest snoring on record is 90 decibels—about the same as a train whistle.

> *There is an often-repeated story about a notorious Texas outlaw, John Wesley Hardin, who once shot and killed a man—for snoring! Hardin was staying at a hotel in Abilene, Texas. The walls of this nineteenth-century hotel were thin, and the man in the next room was snoring loudly—so loudly that Hardin couldn't sleep. So he pulled out his gun, shot through the wall, and killed the man in his bed. Hardin later said he only wanted to quiet the snoring.*

Snoring is one thing, but very loud snorers may actually suffer from sleep apnea. *Apnea* is a Greek word that means "without breath," and one of the symptoms of this sleep disorder is excessively loud snoring. In sleep apnea, the soft tissues of the mouth collapse; and instead of just vibrating and narrowing the passageway for air, they touch each other and completely close it off. It takes about ten seconds, then the brain realizes it isn't getting oxygen and sends out a signal—*Wake up and breathe!* Usually, a person wakes up just enough to gasp for breath. That sound is a loud snorting snore, then the person falls right back to sleep. For a person with sleep apnea, this can happen twenty to sixty times in an hour and ruin a good night's sleep. Like snoring, sleep apnea occurs in adults much more than in children. Fortunately, there are ways to treat the condition.

CHAPTER NINE
Moving Around

MOST PEOPLE GO to sleep when they choose, but there are some who fall asleep when they *don't* choose. It can happen in the middle of a conversation, and even while driving a car or doing some other activity that requires full attention. It's as if they have a "sleep attack." Sometimes the sleep attack lasts for a few seconds, and other times it can last for more than thirty minutes. This type of sleep disorder is called narcolepsy. Doctors are still unsure about the exact cause of narcolepsy. For years, it was thought that an injury to the brain might cause the condition. However, recent studies seem to indicate that a missing neurotransmitter may be interfering with the brain's sleep-wake cycle. Some medications may help with narcolepsy, and doctors are working toward a cure.

Harriet Tubman, the former slave who helped others find freedom through the Underground Railroad, suffered from narcolepsy, sometimes falling asleep as she led people to safety. Harriet Tubman was hit on the head by a cruel slave owner when she was a child. Some think this injury was responsible for her narcolepsy.

Sleepwalking is another strange physical behavior that can occur while sleeping. It is different from RBD, the condition where a person who is dreaming does not experience paralysis and can therefore act out a dream. RBD happens during REM sleep, but sleep researchers know sleepwalking usually takes place during deep, slow-wave sleep. True sleepwalkers are not dreaming. When awakened, people with RBD can describe the dream they were having, but a sleepwalker who is awakened is often confused, even frightened. Like the English girl who climbed the crane, sleepwalkers have no idea how they arrived where they are.

Sleepwalking has sometimes been used as a defense for murder. In Canada, in 1987, a man named Kenneth Parks fell asleep while watching television. Still asleep, he drove his car to his in-laws' house, killed his mother-in-law, and assaulted his father-in-law. Then he drove to the police station and turned himself in. He was asleep the entire time. A jury acquitted him. They believed he really was asleep and didn't know what he was doing.

Like everything else with sleep, sleepwalking remains mysterious, and the causes are unknown. Scientists believe

some people sleepwalk because part of the brain gets a signal from neurotransmitters to "wake up," while the rest of the brain stays asleep. When that part of the brain wakes up, sleepwalking can begin.

Even though these people are sound asleep, their eyes may be open and they stare straight ahead. Sleepwalkers can see, too, even though they are asleep. A sleepwalker can unlock a door—and although their coordination is usually very poor, some sleepwalkers have even driven a car! There have been various reports of people being awakened by the police as they sat in their cars in their pajamas, not having the faintest idea how they came to be where they were.

Children who sleepwalk may just sit up in their beds but not leave them. Others wander around inside the house. However, one young boy left his house wearing only his pajamas and stepped into a few inches of snow—barefoot. He didn't wake up until his father, who had heard the door open, came to carry him back to bed.

Not only do people walk in their sleep, they eat and talk in their sleep, too. One woman said she made salt sandwiches—and ate them—during the night! The evidence of what she had done was on the kitchen counter in the morning when she woke. Others have wakened to find candy and cracker wrappers in their beds.

Back in 1964, New York songwriter Dion McGregor gained a certain amount of fame for his talking in his sleep. Though many people mumble during their sleep, McGregor's voice was clear and easy to understand as he narrated the dreams he was having. In one dream, he described a hot-air-balloon trip to the moon with a group of multi-ethnic children. His sleep talking was so vivid that a roommate recorded him, and his tales were released on a record. It was called *The Dream World of Dion McGregor (He Talks in His Sleep)*.

Some doctors think sleepwalking, sleep talking, sleep eating, and other kinds of bizarre sleep behavior occur when a person is tired from a lack of good, sound sleep—another reason to develop good sleep habits!

CHAPTER TEN
Good Night . . .

ALTHOUGH SCIENCE HAS come a long way since the sleep temples of ancient Greece, there is still a lot to learn about sleep. We can define *sleep* as a physical and mental resting state in which people become partially detached from their world. But we also know that, even while the brain "sleeps," it isn't sleeping. It is always active, in one state or another.

Science has proved that too much, or too little, sleep isn't good for us. But how much is enough? It varies with each person. It is said that Napoleon—and British prime minister Margaret Thatcher—could get along on as little as four hours of sleep a night. But most of us need much more than that. Before the invention of the lightbulb and the clock radio, our great-grandparents went to bed when it got dark, and got up when the rooster crowed in the morning. In those days, people got an average

of nine to ten hours of sleep a night. Today, it is less.

Newborn babies sleep between 16 and 18 hours a day. Young children need between 10 and 12 hours of sleep, and everyone else should be getting between 7 and 9 hours. It's easy to tell if you are getting enough sleep, because if you are, you wake in the morning naturally—no alarm clock, or parent, to shake you out of bed—feeling refreshed and ready to meet the new day.

New research has shown that if you do not get enough sleep, not only will you feel groggy in the morning, your grades in school may actually suffer. One study in Minnesota showed that A students averaged 15 minutes more sleep a night than B students did. B students slept 11 minutes more than C students, and C students snoozed 10 minutes more than the D students did. That's less than an hour's difference between the As and the Ds, but apparently it makes a world of difference on report cards.

The record for going without sleep was set in 1965 by seventeen-year-old Randy Gardner, who went for eleven days without sleep as an experiment for his science fair. While he didn't do himself any permanent damage, after just four days without sleep, he had begun to hallucinate; and by the end he was completely unable to function.

In May 2007, Tony Wright, of Penzance, England, broke his record, but only by a few hours. Wright believed that the left side of the brain (which deals with facts and logic) requires more sleep than the right side (where imagination and feelings are located). He thought that as humans evolved from Stone Age creatures, they began to rely on the left side of their brains more than the right, and therefore needed more sleep. So he consumed a Stone Age diet and tried to use the right side of his brain more than the left, to see if diet and mind control could help him go without sleep.

There is also evidence that not getting enough sleep tends to make a person put on weight. One study suggests that children in elementary school who sleep ten hours at night are more likely to be slim than those who slept for only eight hours. Not getting enough sleep may also be linked to diabetes. Every day our bodies use the carbohydrates we consume to produce blood sugar, or glucose, which gives us energy. Diabetics' bodies have trouble controlling the level of glucose in their blood. Research has shown that not getting enough sleep can slow down the body's ability to process glucose, raising someone's risk for getting this disease.

Lack of sleep can also lead to a condition called hypertension, or high blood pressure. Some studies have shown that just one night without good sleep can result in someone having high blood pressure throughout the following day. If high blood pressure goes untreated over a long period of time, it can eventually lead to heart disease or even a stroke.

So when you go to sleep, you can doze off knowing that even a small amount of extra sleep is great for your health. Our brains and our bodies are wonderful, mysterious creations. Science is still trying to understand all there is to know about them, and though sleep is not fully understood to this day, we now know enough to realize that our brains and bodies both definitely need a good night's sleep.

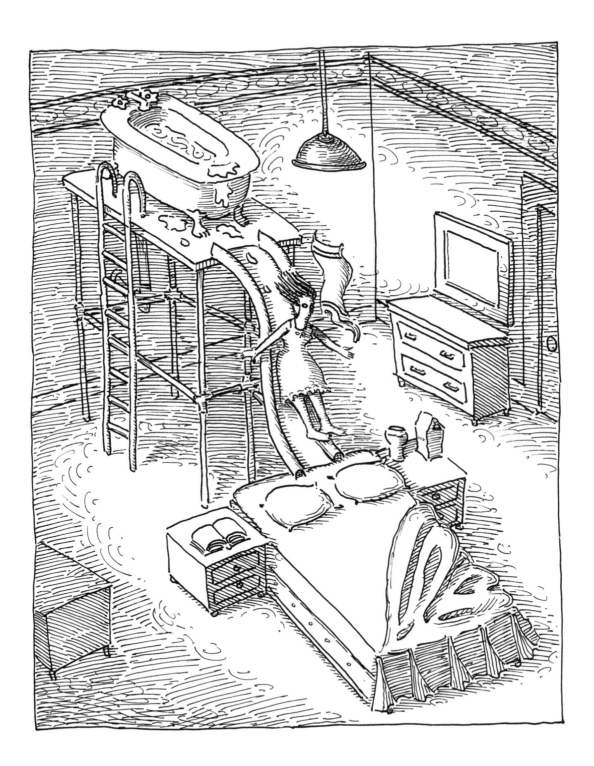

Afterword

PEOPLE TALK ABOUT sleep "habits," because a habit is something that becomes a regular action, or a routine. Eventually, a habit becomes natural behavior. Here are some suggestions to help you develop good sleep habits, so you can get all the benefits of a good night's sleep.

1. Start to relax about thirty minutes before you plan to go to bed. Reading is always a good idea.
2. A glass of milk is helpful, but don't drink any kind of beverage that contains caffeine (this includes dark sodas like colas), because caffeine makes you more alert. In fact, don't drink too much of anything before you go to bed, because you don't want to wake up to use the bathroom.
3. Exercise is good, but you should exercise in the late afternoon, not right before bed.
4. A warm bath helps.
5. And a dark and cool room does, too.
6. If you use a night light, keep it very dim.
7. Relax, breathe deeply, and think of all the good things that happened during the day.

Nighty-night!

Further Reading

Angier, Natalie. "In the Dreamscape of Nightmares, Clues to Why We Dream at All,"
New York Times, October 23, 2007.

Gray, Shirley Wimbish. *Sleeping for Good Health*. Mankato, Minn.: Child's World, 2003.

Schenck, Carlos H., and Bradley V. Baughn, M.D. *Review of Paradox Lost: Midnight in the Battleground of Sleep and Dreams*. Minneapolis: Extreme-Nights LLC, 2005.

Silverstein, Alvin, and Virginia Silverstein. *Sleep*. New York: Franklin Watts, 2000.

"Sleep." www.thinkquest.org/library
ThinkQuest offers student-created sites that provide a comprehensive look at how we sleep, the stages of sleep, sleep disorders, dream symbolism, and how psychologists, including Freud and Jung, look at dreaming.

"Sleep for Kids." www.sleepforkids.org
A service of the National Sleep Foundation, this site answers questions and addresses concerns about sleep and sleep problems. Includes games and puzzles.

Trueit, Trudi Strain. *Dreams and Sleep* (Life Balance). New York: Franklin Watts, 2004.

"What Sleep Is and Why All Kids Need It."
www.kidshealth.org/kid/stay_healthy/body/not_tired.html
KidsHealth! provides doctor-approved information for kids and teens, including information about stages of sleep and a "time for bed" game.

Index